*Nessa*

*scale walls ⸺ ~~~~~~~~~ churches, making out
beautiful brilliant stories every step of the way* [1]
Letter to Violet Dickinson, August 1906
Virginia Stephen

For Virginia Woolf, writing and walking were inextricably linked. She made up her books as she walked along, and much of that walking took place on the South Downs in Sussex. The English countryside surrounded Monk's House, Virginia and Leonard's home, offering peace and solitude, as well as a sense of continuity and replenishment, both vital for her creativity. One of her walks, which she would have done countless times, took her to her sister Vanessa Bell's house, Charleston, in Firle, Lewes.

Using extracts from Virginia's diaries and letters, which record so evocatively her experiences of walking on the Downs, this pamphlet visually reimagines the journey to her sister's house. The artworks are inspired by Virginia's words, as she takes us on an imaginatively expressed but also viscerally felt journey, offering us insight into the spiritually restorative nature of the landscape that she travels through.

At journey's end, Astra Bloom writes movingly about how Virginia Woolf and Monk's House garden offered her solace and healing and the inner strength to begin again in her own life.

Louisa Amelia Albani, 2021, artist, educator & small press publisher

Artwork: left, map of the journey. Louisa Amelia Albani, 2021.
Photo above: Virginia Woolf (née Stephen) and Vanessa Bell playing cricket at Talland House. 1894. Harvard University Library & Vintage Photos of a Young Virginia Woolf Playing Cricket (ages 5 & 12).

*A good week end at Rodmell.. a week end of no talking,*
*sinking at once into deep safe book reading; & then sleep..*
*never a person to be seen, never an interruption:*
*the place to ourselves: the long hours* [2]

Diary entry, Virginia Woolf

Virginia lived at Monk's House in Rodmell, East
Sussex from 1919 until her death in March 1941, a
16th century cottage that would provide the peace
and seclusion she needed for her writing. When
Virginia and Leonard first moved in, there was no
hot water, no bath and no indoor toilet. They added
indoor plumbing and renovated the kitchen,
commissioning Vanessa Bell and Duncan Grant to
design furnishings. Surrounded by the English
countryside and the tranquil garden, Monk's House
became a sanctuary.

*There seemed an infinity of fruitbearing trees;*
*the plums crowded so as to weigh the tip of the branch down;*
*unexpected flowers sprouted among cabbages.*
*There were well kept rows of peas, artichokes, potatoes;*
*raspberry bushes had pale little pyramids of fruit;*
*& I could fancy a very pleasant walk in the orchard*
*under the apple trees*[3]

Diary entry, Virginia Woolf

Although Virginia spoke of her 'pure joy' at spending time in Monk's House garden, working in her writing hut during warmer periods, it was Leonard who became devoted to it. An impressive vegetable patch, ornamental beds, an orchard perfect for sitting under to wile away the hours and ponds filled with rescued fish, he transformed it into a beautiful English garden. In 1928, the Woolfs purchased an adjoining field, thereby preserving their views of the Downs.

Artwork: Louisa Amelia Albani, 2021.

*Sometimes I feel*

*the world desperate;*

*then walk*

*among the Downs* [4]

Diary entry, August 1931,

Virginia Woolf

*Among those primeval downs,*
*like a Heal\* bed L[eonard] said, so comfortable:*
*bowl shaped shadows; half circles; curves; a deep valley*[5]

Diary entry, 1932, Virginia Woolf

Virginia would have been able to see the slopes of
Mount Caburn rising in the distance across the water
meadows of the Ouse Valley. The best preserved
Bronze Age hill fort in Sussex, it's ancient, chalk
downland and south facing slopes attract an
abundance of sun-loving flowers and rare butterflies.
The sweet briar rose, burnt-tip orchids, marjoram,
deep-blue round-headed rampion, tiny chalk milkwort
and horseshoe vetch thrive in this area. Adonis and
chalkhill blue butterflies can also be spotted, as well as
skylarks, meadow pipits, yellowhammers, corn
bunting, kestrels and buzzards.

Artwork: Louisa Amelia Albani, 2021. *Possibly Heals dept store.

The downs breaking their wave,
yet one pale quarry:
& all the barns and stacks
either a broken pink, or a verdurous green;
& then the walk by the wall;
& the church; & the great tithe barn.
How England consoles & warms one,
in these deep hollows,
where the past stands almost stagnant[6]

Diary entry, December 1940
Virginia Woolf

*Here's the sun out for example*
*& all the upper twigs*
*& the trees as if dipped in fire;*
*the trunks emerald green;*
*even bark bright tinted,*
*& variable as the skin of a lizard..*
*The chalk quarry glows pink;*
*& my water meadows lush as June*[7]

Diary entry, January 1920

Virginia Woolf

*&*

*now & then*

*I walk off,*

*miles away,*

*into the downs,*

*find a deserted farm wall,*

*& lie among the thistles*

*& the straw* [8]

Letter to Ethel Smythe, August 1939

Virginia Woolf

*So the summer is ended.. Oh the joy of walking!*

*I've never felt it so strong in me..*

*the trance like, swimming,*

*flying through the air;*

*the current of sensations & ideas;*

*&*

*the slow, but fresh change*

*of down, of road, of colour*[9]

Diary entry, October 1934

Virginia Woolf

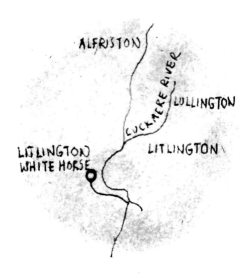

*Blame it or praise it,*
*there is no denying the wild horse in us.*
*To gallop intemperately; fall on the sand tired out;*
*to feel the earth spin;*
*to have — positively — a rush of friendship*
*for stones & grasses, as if humanity were over..*
Virginia Woolf, *Jacob's Room*

Virginia Woolf would have seen impressive views of the Litlington White Horse on her walks across the South Downs. One of two chalk hill figures in East Sussex, it is situated on Hindover Hill with views over the River Cuckmere. There is an evocative photograph of Virginia picnicing with friends on the sloped hillside by the chalked ground.

Artwork: Louisa Amelia Albani, 2021. Photo, right: by DAVID ILIFE. License: CC BY-SA 3.0 (sepia tinted).

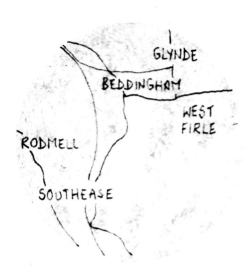

*Yet how the grass shone pale emerald green when I walked off
my temper on the marsh after dinner. The passages of colour,
over Asheham, like the green backgrounds in Vermeer*[10]

Diary entry, Virginia Woolf

Asheham House stood just off the road between
Lewes and Newhaven, near the village of
Beddingham. The Woolfs' country home between
1912 and 1919, they held their wedding party there,
and entertained friends, intellectuals and artists. The
inspiration for Virginia's short story *A Haunted House*
it was a house where, according to Leonard, it seemed
as if each night two people walked from room to
room, opening and shutting doors, sighing,
whispering. It was demolished in 1994.

# ASHEHAM HOUSE *Beddingham*

Photo: Asheham (or Asham) House, near Beddingham, E Sussex. July 1914.

*Imagine the corn*
*all turning different shades of yellow over the downs;*
*& then there's a green patch, & a red one, & so on..* [11]

Letter to Dora Carrington, August 1918
Virginia Woolf

*The look of clouded emerald which the downs wear,*
*the semi-transparent look, as the sun & shadows change,*
*& the green becomes now vivid now opaque* [12]

Diary entry, August 1918
Virginia Woolf

Artwork: Louisa Amelia Albani, 2021.

## MEETING VANESSA

*Virginia Woolf on the path leading to Charleston*

Vanessa Bell (30 May 1879 – 7 April 1961) was an
English painter and interior designer, a member of
the Bloomsbury Group and the sister of Virginia
Woolf. Married to the art critic Clive Bell, in 1916 she
moved to Charleston farmhouse in Firle, with their
two sons Julian and Quentin, where she lived with the
painter and designer Duncan Grant and his lover
David Garnett. Firle was near Asheham and
Virginia had remembered a house she had noticed
there during a walk, which she had mentioned to
Vanessa: an old farmhouse, then a guesthouse, with a
pond in front of it and a walled garden to the side,
close under the Downs.

Artwork: Louisa Amelia Albani, 2021.

# CHARLESTON *the garden*

In her essay on Vanessa Bell and Duncan Grant, Lisa Tickner describes Charleston as 'the house that was also in a sense their masterpiece and joint memorial.'[13] Inspired by the striking colours of Post-Impressionism and stimulated by contact with the Fauves* and Cubists, Vanessa created works that were radical and vibrant, 'a combination of pure, artistic vision and brilliance of imagination'[14] as Virginia put it.

At Charleston, Vanessa and Duncan's artistic talents broke free from their canvases and embellished the walls themselves. In an act of creative regeneration, they invented a style of interior decoration without precedent in British cultural history.

Charleston became a magnet for the Bloomsbury Group, a place where artists, writers, biographers, art historians and economists gathered and shared experimental ideas. Vanessa and Duncan, whose daughter Angelica was born at Charleston, were to live and work there for the rest of their lives.

Artwork: Louisa Amelia Albani, 2021.
*A group of early 20th-century modern artists

## VANESSA BELL at Charleston

*Nessa presides over the most astonishing ménage: Belgian hares,*
*governesses, children, gardeners, hens, ducks, and painting all*
*the time, till every inch of the house is a different colour*[15]
Letter to Violet Dickinson, May 1919
Virginia Woolf

*To many people she appeared frightening and*
*formidable.. I myself never found her formidable,*
*partly because she had the most beautiful speaking voice*
*that I have ever heard, and partly because of*
*her tranquility and quietude.*
*(The tranquility was to some extent superficial;*
*it did not extend deep down in her mind,*
*for there in the depths there was also*
*an extreme sensitivity, a nervous tension)* [16]
Leonard Woolf *on* Vanessa Bell

Artwork: Louisa Amelia Albani, 2021.

On countless days Virginia Woolf walked the 6 miles to Charleston, to visit Vanessa. On her final day, she ended the journey far too soon, at the River Ouse, taking her own life on 28 March 1941.

Contributor Astra Bloom writes movingly about her own illness, and how Virginia Woolf and Monk's House garden offered her solace and healing and the inner strength to begin again.

---

EVERYTHING WAS HEAVY AND THEN THERE WAS COLOUR, LIGHT

In her beautiful essay, *On Being Ill*, published in 1930, Virginia Woolf discusses the fact that illness has never become a prime theme in literature. 'The daily drama of the body,'[17] Woolf points out, has largely gone unrecorded.

Through my own illness I learnt that the body is a precious animal. I find it baffling that we don't bring her suffering, joy and wisdom to the page nearly as often as we should.

I was very ill. For years I could barely walk, stand, sit up even. I became extremely sensitive, to *everything*. One fine hair on my arm felt like scratching wire. A few special places had the power to lift me *just* out of drowning, help me feel less weak, less desperate; one of these blessed locations was Virginia and Leonard Woolf's last home, Monk's House, specifically the cottage garden, beneath which rushed the chalk green river Ouse, the water Virginia stepped into, her pockets full of stones.

On very bad days, I'd ask my husband to take me to Monk's House in Rodmell, it wasn't far from where we lived, and a visit there could make life bearable. Each footstep I took was a triumph. As soon as I was helped out of the car, I would count these steps, whilst trying to remember what normal walking felt like; definitely not this treading on waves, not the ground shifting beneath me as my legs, bones, skin cried out in pain.

But. Gratitude. But Time.
But Magic. But Beauty.

One step. A robin on a nodding peach Hollyhock says *Here, here you are.*
One step. The light through the white Philadelphus hums
*Darling, oh Darling.*
One step. And the Lupins all in a row, flames grown from rich-night-earth,
yellow, mauve,
scarlet, impossibly pink,
tell me, **You** *too can rise tall and burning*
*from what looked like Nothing*
*in what felt like Ending*
*After a long dream of Waiting*
*Out of black so blind and necessary,* **we began again.**

One step. One step.
My bare feet (slipped them off, those sandals like dragged bricks)
on a warm stone path (the one to the right, which I always feel is the best,
because, yes, my little son or daughter will hold my right hand if they
come to be out in the world with me here, instead of sitting on my bed)
and the kindled ground striking teenage memories of Italy, rocks,
my own soft-strong youth into me.

One step. One step.
Up shoot the messages of the earth, Virginia's earth, where she walked,
dreamt, gazed up at birds, or sky and climbing bright life. Spun and spun
voices, worlds, from golden-wing words.

One step.

The path says- *no*, actually the path sings to me,
*It is all waiting, the world is still there, waiting for you.*
*Put down your feet only and all, just as you can;*
*you will not fall.*
*Go slowly as you need, steady as you are able.*
*The future, my darling will come to meet you like a happy dog.*
*Or look, imagine her there, perhaps as a laughing goddess;*
*there at the end of the path, above and below the slice of the blackbirding wing.*
*Through the hedge so neat and gold green,*
*to the shaking long grass, the orchard of straight and slanted trees,*
*the apples, red, yellow, green, once pips, new, naked, buried, sprouting.*

One step. One step.
*Oh, how well you are doing! Now sit here, rest!*
says the brimming Pond of fat gloss orange fish,
lolling sugary lilies snugged with drunken bees,
Magnolia petals, small pages floating on its surface.

And there a white butterfly, and there a red ant,
and in the chestnut the blackbird sings sweet remedies.
And then she speaks. *Does she speak?*
(The veil is thin when you are suffering.)

*Yes.* Here comes Virginia.
China white bones reflected in black silken shade-water.
Oh, how serious, how very candlelit.
In this place of no noise, no pretending.
A garden where illness can exist, can
forge a soul, *may even illuminate it.*

Dear woman, she smiles, waves a hand in the air,
and,
*Time*, Virginia Woolf says.
*This garden, living and dying, flinging on and off her clothes each season;*
*you must soak this all up like sunshine.*
*Then, like the plants, you will grow beyond the moment,*
*outtravel every one of your counted steps.*
*To bloom, be blown about. Fly.*
*Be the colour that catches the eye.*

Astra Bloom writes fiction, poetry and memoir. Her work is published in journals,
magazines and anthologies, including *Common People: an Anthology of Working Class Writers*
and *A Wild and Precious Life* anthology. Astra lives in Brighton and is represented by
Abi Fellows at The Good Literary agency.

# BIBLIOGRAPHY

Andrews, K. *Wanderers: A History of Women Walking* Reaktion Books, 2020.

Anscombe, I. *Omega and After: Bloomsbury and the Decorative Arts* Thames & Hudson, 1981.

Buchan, C. 'The Story Behind the Asham Trust', *Thresholds* 2009–2018.

Chadwick, W, Courtivron, I. *Significant Others: Creativity & Intimate Partnership* Thames & Hudson, 2019.

East Sussex's National Nature Reserves Corporate Report, 2 August 2014.

Gillespie, Diane, F. 'Maps of her own: Virginia Woolf In and Beyond the Archives', *Woolf Studies Annual* Vol. 25, pp. 97–136, Pace University Press, 2019.

Hill-Miller, K. *From the Lighthouse to Monk's House: A Guide to Virginia Woolf's Literary Landscapes* Duckworth, 2001.

Sparks, Elisa, K. 'Woolf on the Downs', 'Woolf and Nature', *Virginia Woolf Miscellany* 81, Spring 2012. Selected Papers from the Twentieth Annual International Conference on Virginia Woolf', 2010.

Woolf, L. *Beginning Again* Harcourt Brace Jovanovich, 1975.

Woolf, V. *Jacob's Room* Oxford World's Classics, 2008.

Woolf, V, *On Being Ill* Paris Press, 2002.

Woolf, V. *The Diary of Virginia Woolf* 5 Vols, Ed. Olivier Bell, A, with the assistance of McNellie, A. New York, Harcourt Brace, 1977–1984.

Woolf, V. *The Letters of Virginia Woolf* 6 Vols, Ed. Nicolson, N, Trautmann, J. New York, Harcourt, 1975–80.

REFERENCES

[1] Woolf, V, I, p. 234, *The Letters of Virginia Woolf*
[2] Woolf, V, IV, p. 109, *The Diary of Virginia Woolf*
[3] Woolf, V, I, pp. 286-7, *The Diary of Virginia Woolf*
[4] Woolf, V, IV, p. 39, *The Diary of Virginia Woolf*
[5] Woolf, V, IV, p. 74, *The Diary of Virginia Woolf*
[6] Woolf, V, V, p. 346, *The Diary of Virginia Woolf*
[7] Woolf, V, II, pp. 3-4, *The Diary of Virginia Woolf*
[8] Woolf, V, VII, p. 352, *The Letters of Virginia Woolf*
[9] Woolf, V, IV, p. 246, *The Diary of Virginia Woolf*
[10] Woolf, V, V, p. 301, *The Diary of Virginia Woolf*
[11] Woolf, V, II, p. 267, *The Letters of Virginia Woolf*
[12] Woolf, V, I, p. 185, *The Diary of Virginia Woolf*
[13] Chadwick, W, Courtivron, I, p. 63, *Significant Others*
[14] Woolf, V, III, p. 164, *The Letters of Virginia Woolf*
[15] Woolf, V, *The Letters of Virginia Woolf*
[16] Woolf, L, p. 27, *Beginning Again*
[17] Woolf, V, p. 4, *On Being Ill*